HALLOWEEN DAD JOKES

Devin Parker

ISBN-13: 9781234567890
ISBN-10: 1477123456

Library of Congress Control Number: 2018675309
Printed in Canada

This book is dedicated to my wonderful parents and my social media audience that appreciate my constant dad jokes.

CONTENTS

DISCLAIMER

This book is just regular dad jokes. It is not actually holiday themed and is perfect for any time of year! (Except fathers day)

THE ONLY CHAPTER

The first joke of the day is me... The author.

The Second joke is you.

Okay, now let's get to the real knee slappers.

Q: How can you tell when the moon is broke?

A: When it's down to it's last quarter!

◆ ◆ ◆

Q: How do you get into Canadian Universities?

A: You're gonna need straight eh's!

Q: What is a writers blood type?

A: Type-O!

◆ ◆ ◆

Q: What do you get when you mix alcohol and literature?

A: Tequilla mockingbird!

◆ ◆ ◆

Q: How do you organize a party in outerspace?

A: You planet!

◆ ◆ ◆

Q: What do you call crows that stick together?

A: Velcro!

◆ ◆ ◆

Q: What do you call an alligator in a vest?

A: An investigator!

◆ ◆ ◆

Q: What do you call a laughing jar of mayonaise?

A: LMAO!

Q: When does a joke become a dad joke?

A: When it becomes apparent!

◆ ◆ ◆

Q: Why did karen hit Ctrl+Shift+Delete?

A: She wanted to see the task manager!

◆ ◆ ◆

Q: Why did the old man fall in the well?

A: He couldn't see that well!

◆ ◆ ◆

Q: How does a non-binary samurai kill people?

A: They slash them! (They/Them)

◆ ◆ ◆

Q: Why do melons have weddings?

A: Because they cantaloupe!

◆ ◆ ◆

Q: What do sprinters eat before a race?

A: Nothing, they fast...

◆ ◆ ◆

Q: Why is diarrhea hereditary?

A: Because it runs in your jeans!

◆ ◆ ◆

Q: What generation does Forest Gump belong to?

A: Gen-A

◆ ◆ ◆

Q: What do you call a small mother?

A: A minimum!

◆ ◆ ◆

Q: what do painters do when they get cold?

A: They put on another coat!

◆ ◆ ◆

Q: What's the difference between you and a calender?

A: A calender has dates.

◆ ◆ ◆

Q: how does a computer get drunk?

A: It takes screenshots!

◆ ◆ ◆

Q: How does the moon cut its hair?

A: Eclipse it!

◆ ◆ ◆

Q: What do you call someone with no body

and no nose?

A: Nobody Knows!

◆ ◆ ◆

Q: what do you call a man with no shins?

A: Tony!

◆ ◆ ◆

Q: What do you call a fish that eats bums?

A: A bottom feeder

◆ ◆ ◆

Q: What do you call a man with a rubber toe?

A: Roberto!

◆ ◆ ◆

Q: What do you call batman when he is injured?

A: Bruised Wayne!

◆ ◆ ◆

Q: Why are bakers so rich?

A: Because they make so much dough!

Q: What do you call a bear with no teeth?

A: A gummy bear!

◆ ◆ ◆

Q: What do you call a dinosaur with a great vocabulary?

A: A thesaurus

◆ ◆ ◆

Q: What do you call an acid with an attitude?

A: A Mean-o-acid!

◆ ◆ ◆

Q: What do you call James Bond in a bathtub?

A: Bubble 07

◆ ◆ ◆

Q: What did the Sushi say to the bee?

A: Wasabi!

Q: Why did the Mexican take anti-anxiety medication?

A: For hispanic attacks.

◆ ◆ ◆

Q: What kind of shoes do ninjas wear?

A: Sneakers...

◆ ◆ ◆

Q: How do billboards talk to each other?

A: Sign language.

◆ ◆ ◆

Q: Why couldn't the toilet paper cross the road?

A: It got stuck in a crack!

◆ ◆ ◆

Q: What kind of bees produce milk?

A: boobies!

◆ ◆ ◆

Q: Where does someone go if they get hurt playing peekaboo?

A: To the I see you!

◆ ◆ ◆

Q: What did 20 do when it was hungry?

A: 28

◆ ◆ ◆

Q: What did Yoda say when he saw himself in 4K?

A: HDMI

◆ ◆ ◆

Q: Why does spidermans calender only have 11 months?

A: He lost May.

❖ ❖ ❖

Q: What are the strongest days?

A: Saturday and Sunday, the rest are weekdays.
Q: What do you get when you eat too many edibles?

A: A pot belly.

❖ ❖ ❖

Q: What do ticks and the Eiffel tower have in common?

A: They're both Paris sites!

❖ ❖ ❖

Q: What did 50 Cent do when he got hungry?

A: 58

❖ ❖ ❖

Q: What pronoun does chocolate go by?

A: Hershey

◆ ◆ ◆

Q: How does a pilot take his sandwich?

A: Plane

Q: What do you call a group of rabbits walking backwards?

A: A receding hairline

◆ ◆ ◆

Q: Why do fathers take an extra sock with them when they go golfing?

A: In case the get a hole in one!

◆ ◆ ◆

Q: What do you call a factory that makes okay products?

A: A satisfactory.

◆ ◆ ◆

Q: Where do fruits go on vacation?

A: Pear-is

◆ ◆ ◆

Q: What has more letters than the alphabet?

A: The post office

Q: What do you call a poor Santa Claus?

A: St. Nickel-less!

◆ ◆ ◆

Q: What did one hat say to the other?

A: Stay here! I'm going on ahead...

◆ ◆ ◆

Q: Why can't a nose be 12 inches long?

A: Because then it would be a foot.

◆ ◆ ◆

Q: What kind of car does an egg drive?

A: A yolkswagon.

◆ ◆ ◆

Q: How do you make 7 even?

A: Take away the s

Q: What country's capital is growing the fastest?

A: Ireland. Every day it's Dublin.

◆ ◆ ◆

Q: Why can't you hear a pterodactyl take a piss?

A: Because the P is silent!

◆ ◆ ◆

Q: What do you get from a pampered cow?

A: Spoiled milk!

◆ ◆ ◆

Q: What is the best smelling insect?

A: A deodor-ant!

◆ ◆ ◆

Q: What does garlic do when it gets too hot?

A: It takes some cloves off.

Q: What is a computers favorite snack?

A: Computer chips.

◆ ◆ ◆

Q: What is an astronauts favorite part of a computer?

A: The space bar.

◆ ◆ ◆

Q: What's the leading cause of dry skin?

A: Towels

◆ ◆ ◆

Q: What do you call bears without ears?

A: B.

◆ ◆ ◆

Q: What do you call it when a car writes it's life story?

A: An autobiography

Q: Where should you work if you want to tell people their fortunes?

A: The bank!

◆ ◆ ◆

Q: Why do ghosts like to eat healthy food so much?

A: Because it's supernatural!

◆ ◆ ◆

Q: What's a witches favorite subject?

A: Spelling.

◆ ◆ ◆

Q: What has four wheels and flies?

A: A garbage truck.

Q: Why is it impossible to play hide-and-seek with Pokemon?

A: Because they always Pikachu

◆ ◆ ◆

Q: Why is Peterpan always flying?

A: Because he neverlands!

◆ ◆ ◆

Q: What is the easiest way to get straight A's?

A: Use a ruler.

◆ ◆ ◆

Q: How do scientists keep their breath fresh?

A: Experimints!

◆ ◆ ◆

Q: Why does it take pirates so long to learn the alphabet?

A: Because they spend years at C!

Q: Why did the duck fall in love with the dog?

A: It was pure bread!

◆ ◆ ◆

Q: Why did the clock get kicked out of the library?

A: It tocked too much.

◆ ◆ ◆

Q: Why did the frog make fun of the toad?

A: To rib it.

◆ ◆ ◆

Q: Where can you always find a date?

A: A calendar!

◆ ◆ ◆

Q: If a reindeer lost its tail, where would it go for a new one?

A: The retail store!

Q: Where do Santa's elves keep their money?

A: In a snow bank.

◆ ◆ ◆

Q: Why do cows have bells?

A: In case their horns don't work.

◆ ◆ ◆

Q: How does a walrus know what is good to eat?

A: There's a seal of approval.

◆ ◆ ◆

Q: Why are football stadiums so cool?

A: Because every seat has a fan in it!

◆ ◆ ◆

Q: How do you keep warm in a cold room?

A: You go to the corner, because it's always

90 degrees.

Q: What kind of cat never tells the truth?

A: A lion.

◆ ◆ ◆

Q: Why don't elephants use computers?

A: They're too afraid of the mouse.

◆ ◆ ◆

Q: What is Forest gumps password?

A: 1Forest1

◆ ◆ ◆

Q: Why do people wear shamrocks on St. Patricks Day?

A: Because real rocks are too heavy.

◆ ◆ ◆

Q: How do trees access the internet?

A: They log on.

Q: Why was the cheetah so bad at hide-and-seek?

A: No matter where it hid, it was always spotted.

◆ ◆ ◆

Q: What's orange and sounds like a parrot?

A: A carrot

◆ ◆ ◆

Q: What do you call an empty jar of cheese wiz?

A: Cheese was.

◆ ◆ ◆

Q: What kind of horses only come out after dark?

A: Nightmares.

Q: Why is maple syrup so romantic?

A: It can't help it, it's sappy!

◆ ◆ ◆

Q: What is a pigs favorite karate move?

A: A pork chop!

◆ ◆ ◆

Q: If a firefighter has two eyes, then what does a ballerina have?

A: Two too.

◆ ◆ ◆

Q: Which horse runs the city?

A: The mare of course!

◆ ◆ ◆

Q: What type of nails do carpenters hate to hammer?

A: Fingernails.

Q: Why did the kid eat his homework?

A: His teacher told him it was a piece of cake.

◆ ◆ ◆

Q: What did the vinaigrette say to the refrigerator?

A: Close the door! I'm dressing!

◆ ◆ ◆

Q: Why are libraries so strict?

A: They have to go by the book.

CHAPTER 2
(I LIED)

Okay so chapter 1 as you have noticed, is Q&A jokes. Chapter 2 will be one liners.

1) I went to the zoo the other week and it was just one animal. It was one dog alone in a cage...
It was a Shih tzu.

2) Have you heard about the new anti-gravity book? Apparently you can't put it down!

3) I love telling dad jokes. Sometimes he even laughs!

4) I saw a radio on sale the other day, ad said:

"$1 volume stuck on full blast."
I couldn't turn it down.

5) Did you hear the rumor about butter? I'm not gonna spread it...

6) Ran out of toilet paper this morning, so i've been using old newspaper.
The Times are tough.

7) I called work this morning and whispered, "Sorry boss, I can't come in today. I have a wee cough.
He exclaimed, "You have a wee cough?"
I said, "Really? Thanks boss, see you next week!

8) I'm giving my chimney away for free.
You could say it's on the house...

9) My doctor told me I was going deaf.
The news was hard for me to hear...

10) I hate my job, all I do is crush cans all day...
It's soda pressing.

11) My drug dealer cracks me up.

12) I'm gonna start doing lunges to stay in shape.
That'd be a big step forward.

13) Did you hear about that kidnapping at school?
It's okay, he woke up...

14) I only know 25 letters of the alphabet...
I don't know y

15) I don't trust stairs.
They're always up to something...

16) Never trust an atom.
They make up everything!

17) I want to visit a Scandinavian country but there's Norway I could a-fjord to go there.

18) I went to the zoo and saw a baguette in a cage.
It was bread in captivity.

19) I named my horse Mayo.

Sometimes Mayo neighs.

20) My wife bet me $100 that I couldn't turn spaghetti into a car.
You should have seen her face when I drove pasta!

21) Today was my sons fourth birthday party. I didn't recognize him at first.
I've never seen him be four.

22) I taught my pet wolf how to meditate. Now he's aware wolf.

23) I had a good childhood, my dad used to roll me down hills in tires.
Those were goodyears.

24) I'm not saying that I am attractive, but everytime I go into the bathroom and take my clothes off, I turn the shower on.

25) An invisible man married an invisible woman.
Their children were nothing to look at either.

26) Did you know that the first french fries were not cooked in France?
They were cooked in grease.

27) My wife told me that quilts are better than duvets.
I told her that she better be careful making blanket assumptions like that.

28) My wife told me that the salads I make tend to be on the dry side.
Definitely something that needs a-dressing.

29) My wife told me that I had no sense of direction.
So I asked her where that came from.

30) My dog accidently ate a whole bag of scrabble tiles, so I took him to the vet.
No word yet.

31) I got fired from the bank today after a woman asked me to check her balance.
I pushed her.

32) My wife said she could list 14 reason why she could leave me, including my love

for tennis.
I said "That's 15 honey"

33) If money doesn't grow on trees, then why do banks have branches?

34) Yesterday I opened my water and electric bill at the same time.
I was shocked.

35) If you think gas and electricity costs are expensive, you should see chimneys.
They're through the roof.

36) I asked my wife to rate my listening skills.
She said "You're an 8 on a scale of 10"
No idea why she wants me to piss on a skeleton.

37) I warned my kids about using the whistle inside the house.
I gave them one last warning.
They blew it...

38) My wife said she looked fat and asked if I could give her a compliment.
I told her that she had perfect eyesight.

39) I hate when my wife gets mad at me for being lazy.
It's not like I did anything.

40) If 666 is all evil, then 25.8069758 is the root of all evil.

41) I asked my friend Sam to sing a song about the iphone.
So Samsung.
42) Is buttcheeks one word? Or should I spread them apart?

43) I tried catching fog the other day.
Mist.

44) Do they allow loud laughing in Hawaii?
Or just a low ha.

45) I just crashed my new KIA
Now I have noKIA

46) The Egyptians claim there are no crocodiles in their country.
I think they're in de Nile...

47) I asked my wife when her birthday was.
She said March 1st.
So I walked around the room and asked her again.

48) I started a class to teach math to midgets.
I like to make the little things count.

49) I'm worried about the calender.
It's days are numbered...

50) I thought the dryer was shrinking my clothes.
Turns out it was the refrigerator...

51) Dear Math, grow up and solve your own problems.

52) I only know 25 letters of the alphabet.
I don't know y.

53) This graveyard looks overcrowded.
People must be dying to get in.

54) That car looks nice, but that muffler looks exhausted!

55) Shout out to my fingers.
I can count on all of them.

56) I had a dream I was floating in an ocean of orange soda.
Actually, it was more of a fanta sea.

57) I got fired from the canned juice company. Apparently I couldn't concentrate.

58) People say they pick their nose but I dunno...
I was born with mine.

59) I love telling dad jokes. Sometimes he even laughs.

60) People think icy is the easiest word to spell.
Come to think of it, I see why.

61) A clown held the door for me today.
That was a nice jester.

62) Every psychic I have ever met is either

hopelessly romantic or all doom and gloom.
Why can't I find a happy medium?

63) Don't even get me started on velcro.
What a rip off.

64) To the person who stole my glasses:
I will find you.
I have contacts.

65) The sporting goods store just had abig
sale on canoes.
It was quite the oar deal.
66) How about a frozen joke?
I couldn't think of anything Elsa... let it go.

67) When the librarian bumped her head,
she had no one to blame but her shelf.

68) People are shocked when they find out
i'm not a very good electrician.

69) Nice

70) I thought I spotted a leopard once.
Turns out they're born like that.

71) A burglar stole all my lamps.
I should be upset, but i'm delighted.

72) whiteboards are quite remarkable.

73) My friend just got a job playing hard in an orchestra.
She had to pull a few strings.

74) Never confide in a vacuum cleaner.
They're always gathering dirt.

75) The phrase don't you dare is an abbreviation for do not you dare.

76) Is it just me, or is ever other number... odd?

77) The smartest tool to have is a thermometer.
It has so many degrees.

78) Did you hear about the man who lost the right side of his bottom?
Apparently it was just left behind.

79) My friend can't figure out what video

game console to get and he's kind of upset about it.
Nobody can console him.

80) To the person who stole my coffee, my lamp, and my parrot:
I don't know how you sleep at night.

81) The right eye said to the left eye, "Between you and me, something smells"

WRITE YOUR OWN
JOKES DOWN

ABOUT THE AUTHOR

Devin Parker

Devin parker is a Scifi and fantasy author that is also an avid lover of puns and dad jokes.

If you want to check out his other work, you can go to amazon and search:

A New Sky by Devin J Parker (Book 1)

or

The Lost City by Devin J Parker

You can also follow me on Tiktok, Youtube, Instagram and Twitter by searching the usernames:

Gamewrites

and

Writing with Devin J Parker

A THANK YOU FROM THE AUTHOR

I hope you enjoyed reading this silly book as much as I enjoyed writing it!

Thank you to everyone that reads this book and any of my fiction books. You guys are the best!

Also pineapple belongs on pizza.